A BALKAN BYZANTINE NOTEBOOK

Drawings by
Catharine Phillips Fels

Text by
Carl Sheppard

Carnelian Press, Taos, New Mexico, 1990

ISBN 0-9623155-0-8

Library of Congress Catalog Card Number 88-92899

Title Page and Cover: Capital, Basilica "B," Philppi

Carnelian Press
PO Box 3165, Taos, New Mexico   87571

CONTENTS

PREFACE

Many years ago I was Carl Sheppard's teaching assistant. He led me to begin to understand what style is through a question on an exam that I graded. He showed some slides and asked the students to answer three questions about them. Specific identification was not expected. All were obscure. The questions were: From what place? From what time? and What is the style? (of the work of art)

One was an early medieval Slavic relief. I jotted down my answer "Yugoslav and early medieval." The first because it resembled Mestrovitch's Stations of the Cross in a Chicago church, the second from its state of preservation and religious content. I said the style was expressionist, which I still think is correct although with wider acquaintance with Mestrovitch I realize that his work is not always expressionist.

I am happy and grateful that Carl Sheppard agreed to write, however briefly, about these buildings that I found so much pleasure in drawing. He is familiar with most of them, especially those in Greece, Turkey, and Yugoslavia. He is a distinguished medievalist. His opinions and information are impeccable. Perhaps more clearly than any other art form, architecture, buildings, tell us what sort of people used them. My introduction to this understanding came from Carl Sheppard.

Why does a specific age or style or language or, in my case, architecture so take one's imagination that beyond any practical purpose one finds a large piece of one's life devoted to it? I can't say why. If I could I would be able to explain all the eccentric professors I've known.... and loved, if only for their books.

Whyever it came about, my pleasure in drawing the buildings pictured here was keen. In drawing them I learned them. Ross Parmenter says of this experience: "The doorway (in his drawing) looks more beautiful on paper than it did in fact. This puzzled me.... then I realized I had put the cart before the horse. It was not that I had drawn the doorway more beautiful than it was but previously I had not recognized the degree of the portal's beauty."

The drawings are the product of a love affair that grew as the pile of drawings grew. My husband, Leonard Fels, was truly generous not only in accompanying me to Italy, Greece, Turkey, Romania and Yugoslavia but also in photographing the buildings as I was drawing. Diverting the children who inevitably crowd around was a valuable contribution, too.

It is at least partly in appreciation for Leonard Fels that I put this volume together. He gave several whole summers over to Byzantine travels and became quite a Byzantine affecianado himself.

I am especially indebted to Halil and Mergube Göknil of Bebek, Istanbul. They shared generously their considerable knowledge of their city and its history. They gave us the notes we gave to taxi drivers and conductors that eased our travels in Istanbul. Barbara Massey was a fine companion in Yugoslavia in 1969. In 1980, I returned to northern Greece and Yugoslavia with my sister Claribel Johnson and my friend Edyse Hoffman. My granddaughter Abigail Palmer went on this exursion and also worked at the dig in Andravida in 1983.

During my 1970 fellowship at the Helene Wurlitzer Foundation of New Mexico, I worked on this project. My thanks to Henry Sauerwein, the Director. He also taught me the four or five words of Bulgarian that contributed to my survival in Nessebar.

I received many kindnesses from friends, friends of friends, and strangers, too. Far too many to list. I am nevertheless truly grateful.

C.P.F., Taos, 1988.

INTRODUCTION

Catharine Phillips Fels was born and grew up in the middle-west. She spent most of her adult life in California, where she had many exhibitions and taught until retirement as Professor Emerita at California State University, Los Angeles. With her husband, Leonard, who was Professor of Philosophy at Long Beach State University, she traveled intermittently for three decades over the eastern Mediterranean, especially in Turkey, Yugoslavia and Romania.

She now lives in Taos, New Mexico, where her energies are directed toward painting local landscape. In winter she visits the Yucatan and paints there.

Catharine last visited the Balkans in 1984. She accepted the position as an artist with the Minnesota-Andravida Project and worked in 1983 and 1984 at the Cathedral of Andravida. After her duties there, she continued to Istanbul where she attended the opening of an exhibition of her paintings of Seljuk buildings, made in Turkey, Iran and Soviet Azerbaijan. Although this "Notebook" is exclusively taken up with Byzantine architecture, a second love of Catharine's is Islamic architecture of Asia Minor and the Balkans. Most of her pictures of this material are, however, in gouache or watercolor, not pen and ink. The countries of the Balkans have fascinated Catharine, who has not excluded any aspect of the complicated history of the region from her interest.

To Americans, unless they have ethnic roots there, this region is exotic. The great peninsula IS. Although sharing the Judeo-Christian heritage of Rome with the West, the Balkan area from the fifth century, developed its own version of that civilization. Constantinople was for a thousand years the cultural and political center of the Roman Empire. It represents one of the three great descendants of Rome: The Latin West, the Greek East and the Islamic South. Westerners are probably now more familiar with the Islamic world than with the Greek. Westerners and Easterners have always cherished competition between themselves. The competition involved revealed religious truth, social status, and economic wellbeing. The attitudes of the United States and Russia toward each other parallel the animosities that have raged between the Catholic West and the Orthodox East. After Constantinople fell to the Turks in 1453, Moscow proclaimed itself successor to the fallen city as the third Rome.

Invasions, conversions, violent political upheavals, all have made the Balkan peninsula a most complex place. From any point of view the area is very mixed up. However, with the exception of Dalmatia, the culture has been predominantly Byzantine.... a fact particularly evident in its architecture.

Mistrust, wild tales of danger and strangeness of language have kept the Balkans relatively free of Western travelers. Only the hearty and intrepid and very curious have ventured there except for those who took the Oriental Express through to Istanbul.... the modern name for Constantinople, the name that superceded Byzantium.

Catharine perceived the Balkans with an artist's eye, i.e. she interpreted what she saw by drawing it, transferring the forms of architecture to equivalents in pen and ink. Instead of the usual and anticipated report on plains, valleys, mountains, vegetation and urban picturesque scenes, we are presented with an architectural record.

It is a record, however, that is selective of those buildings most sacred to the people at each site. These buildings have survived and represent continuity through more than four centuries of

Islamic political superiority. Each church implies a culture continuous since 330 a.d., the year the Emperor Constantine moved the capital of Rome to the shores of the Bosphorus.

Byzantium was a Greek city located on a peninsula held between the Sea of Marmora, the narrow passage of the Bosphorus, which is Turkish for gullet, and the estuary of a small river. It was here that the first phase of the religious architecture of the peninsula developed its Christian heritage. The Empire considered itself Roman at that time and until it perished it was always Rome to its subjects. Romania still carries the name as does the European portion of modern Turkey, Rumelia. It was not until the ninth century that Rome, or Byzantium as we now refer to the Empire, coalesced into a new cultural and political entity. New Rome had lost the southern Mediterranean and Palestine to the Arabs; the West had been taken by barbarian tribes from the north and east. A good deal of the Balkans was also lost, including Greece, to occupation by Slavs, Avars, Bulgarians and Magyars. For brief intervals all that remained were islands of the Aegean and Adriatic and the great metropolis itself.

By the ninth century Byzantium had become identifiable: Greek had replaced Latin, Orthodox Christianity had developed its own theology, and Constantinople had unified herself geographically over Asia Minor and the Balkans.

The first phase of Byzantine architecture, often referred to as the First Golden Age, is elegant. It was built largely during the reigns of the Emperor Justinian and the Empress Theodora in the sixth century. The Roman Empire was experiencing a time of prosperity and the Emperor spent lavishly on structures that brought prestige wherever they were built and for the institutions that used them. The surviving buildings show a continuation of the great Roman tradition of engineering with concrete and brick or stone. Where possible large size was encouraged by the central authorities as were luxurious furnishings: mosaics, frescoes, silk and cotton curtains and other rich articles. There was a tendency to centralize creating a psychological effect so that mind or soul moved upward into the dome of heaven in the context of revealed religion.

The second phase of Byzantine architecture dates from the ninth century to the traitorous capture of the capital by the Crusaders in 1204.

The Latin Empire which resulted lasted until 1259 when the Greeks succeeded in taking the city. They held it until the Turks took it in 1453. The third great florescence of Byzantine architecture of which many examples are to be found in present-day Yugoslavia and Greece, as well as in Istanbul itself, dates from this period. More history will be forthcoming as it seems important to the explanation of particular buildings.

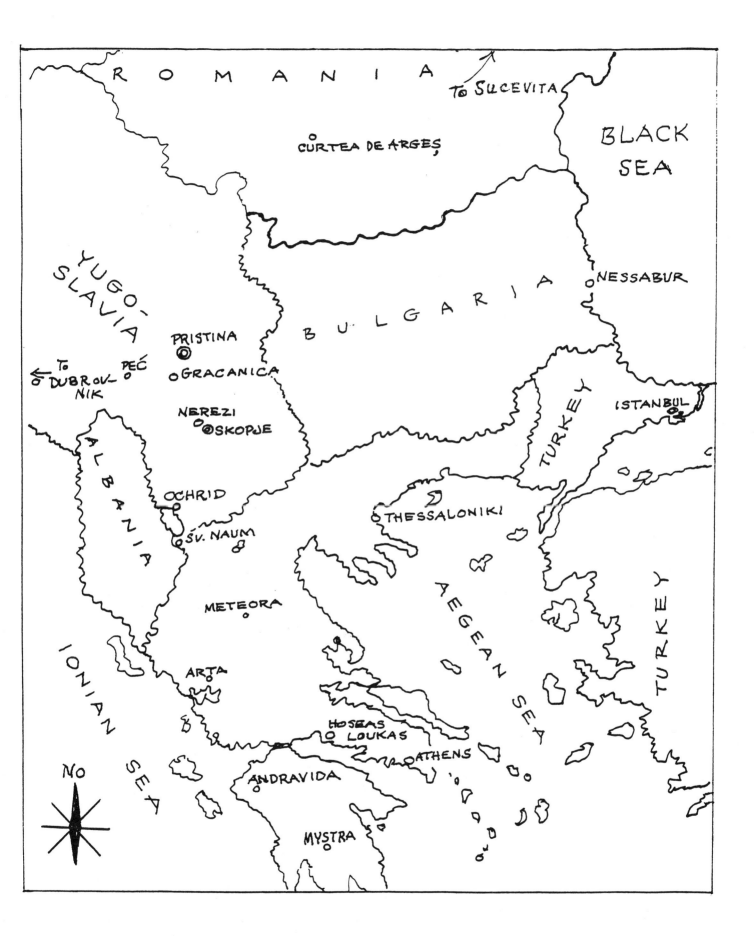

TURKEY

ISTANBUL

The First Byzantine Golden Age

The greatest building ever constructed in the Byzantine Empire is the Church dedicated to Holy Wisdom, The Word of God, The Logos, Haghia Sophia, at Constantinople. Its construction was ordered by the Emperor Justinian after the Nike riots. It was built between 532 and 537 by the architects Anthemius of Tralles and Isidore of Miletus. No other structure in the world had such a vast uninterrupted interior space until modern steel and concrete materials made it possible. It would cost at least a billion American dollars to duplicate it now and a lot more to furnish it as it was originally. This is pointed out merely to indicate how important Hagia Sophia was to the Empire.

It was the church of the Patriarch, the highest religious figure in the state, and stood on a great square with the Palace of the Emperor, the Senate and the Palace of the Patriarch. Near its entrance was the marker from which all distances to points in the Empire were measured. Hagia Sophia was the soul of the state. The Emperor, who was above the Patriarch in authority, could also officiate at various ceremonies in the Megala Ecclesia, as it came to be called. It became a mosque in 1453 and a museum under the regime of Attaturk in the 1930s.

When asked to describe her experiences of Istanbul, Catharine wrote as follows:

> We were warned of dangers, misunderstandings
> Fascination prevailed. Love of the ancient, the buried, the
> > conquered, the drowned.
> The fabled city, turquoise waters around
> Asia beyond the swift current
> Flowing from the sea called Black.
> They are cruel, hard, tough, ignorant and harsh, we were told.
> But their voices were sweet as they called to one another
> Up and down the old staircase that squeaked since it was pegged,
> > not nailed.

In the foyer was a grandmother's cradle filled with potted plants
On the floor the finest carpet and a great brass brazier.
Old things, family-loved things.
Of the great church they said 'Christian churches are dark and gloomy'
They could not see the gold and silver screens, the gilded lamps
Soft glowing icons and thousands of candles, no longer there.
They stood in line politely, took turns boarding bus and trolley.
'I had two mothers-in-law,' said one. 'In my family
There were no plural marriages for three hundred years'
Said another. I could hardly say as much.... I don't know.
'My father rode with my mother and sisters as if for an
                    afternoon call, but he carried gold.
He was the Sultan's Visier but he took the gold to Attaturk.'
'My father went with him to Smyrna. He never returned.'
Their voices spell the "him" with a capital.
Food is dainty and elegant. 'This was my grandmother's cake recipe.'
'Mrs. Thurston taught me to bake this cake.'
'An Armenian taught me this or that... They are our best cooks.'
The dishes used by the Sultan are in Topkapi Serai.
Miles of shelves and cupboards full of celadon from China.
Palest sea green.

Catharine continues: "We set out every morning with notes from our hosts to give to trolley, bus or taxi driver, to get us to our objectives. We often had lunch in the city and went on to a museum or back to our morning site. We tried to start back to Bebek (a small town up the Bosphorus, a favorite residence for foreigners) by three o'clock as at that time a cool breeze comes down the Bosphosus from the Black Sea, making the ride home more pleasant. I often worked more on the drawings in the evening while the building was still fresh in my mind.

Hagia Sophia, Istanbul, from the southeast ⟹

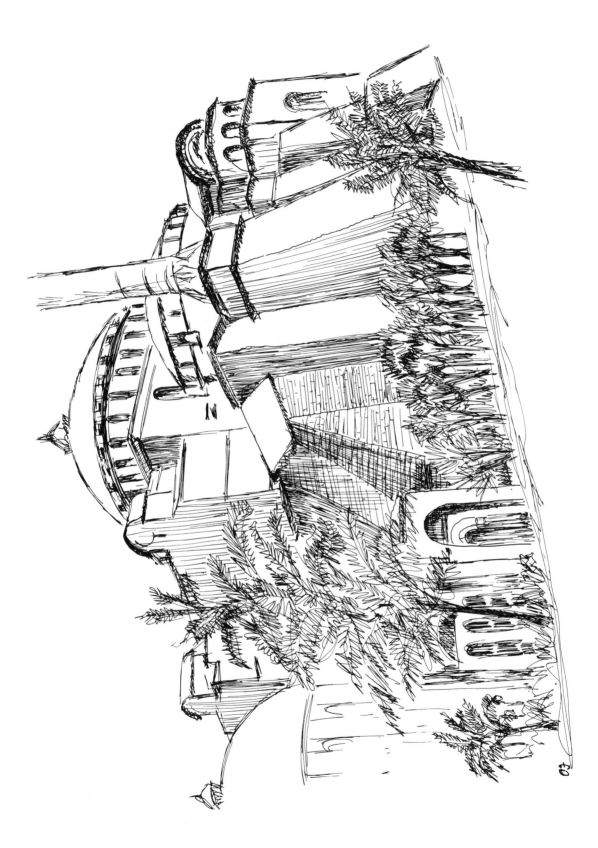

"We went to Hagia Sophia on our first morning in Istanbul but the Shah of Iran was there before us and no one else was allowed in. I did go to the Archaeological Office in front and obtained a letter giving me permission to draw in the city. We set off down the slope towards the Palace Mosaics (now a museum) and Kücük Hagia Sophia (originally Saints Sergius and Bacchus). I was able to draw inside Kücük Hagia Sophia and everyone who knows is amazed as it is in use as a mosque. I suspect the caretaker couldn't read my paper, but it got me in with chair, paper, and pens, as it did to Feneri Isa and Calendar Cami, now museums but at that time undergoing restoration and closed to visitors."

Hagia Sophia, Istanbul

As Catharine did not draw many views of the exterior of Hagia Sophia we need a little history. Indeed, except possibly from the east, the church has suffered so much alteration on the outside as to discourage investigation. The structure of brick and cement went up so quickly that the masonry did not have time to dry or cure. The galleries were not yet completed when the building began to sag. The floors of the galleries were like the surfaces of lakes agitated by light winds. Since that time many restorations have sustained the great church; the exterior, however, no longer indicates the brilliance of the interior.

"I must have spent nearly two months in and around Hagia Sophia. It interests me infinitely. We went there so often that the guards knew us. Lenny read in the garden while I drew inside. One guard said to Lenny, 'You're a lucky man. You don't have to worry about your wife. She just wants to draw.' Once we were bewildered by a handsome young man who stopped us on the street, slapped Lenny on the back and shook my hand. We didn't recognize the guard out of uniform.

"The building began to seem to me like some great natural phenomenon, different at different times of day and moody according to the weather. I brought a little folding chair and sat inside. I usually drew inside and painted outside. After the Pope's visit in 1967, I painted inside as the color was wonderful after the marble revetment had been washed. The black iron lamps were gilded at the same time, making the whole building seem lighter. The differences between morning and afternoon light inside Hagia Sophia are great. The northeast gallery is delicate in the morning light. Afternoon light changes the west galleries.

Hagia Sophia, Istanbul, interior, view to the north and east   ⟹

"Though I know something about the uses of Hagia Sophia's, I gave this very little attention. I was absorbed by the visual relationships, spaces, textures, and colors. I did, of course, wonder whether there were mosaics behind plaster. Once I began drawing or painting the problems that are present became all absorbing. I don't usually forget what I've drawn.... occasionally I don't recall where a passage is, but I recall it perfectly.

"With regard to drawings: On the whole, I didn't make any pencil guidelines, at least very rarely. If I needed construction lines, they are there with a fine pen line. My idea was that the directly drawn line, fresh, made while looking at the subject, has the most life. I did very little correction on the theory that my first reaction was the strongest and clearest. Sometimes a drawing just didn't 'go.' In that case, I threw it away and started over. Where, rather rarely, I did correct and a darker spot appeared in the drawing, I later used a little white-out... not often.

"When I first arrived in Berkeley in 1931, the DeYoung Museum in San Francisco had an exhibition of Russian Icons. I'd never seen any paintings like them and I was fascinated. Though very few people see it, since most of my work is recognizable in subject and I usually use conventional perspective, much of my painting technique derives from icons. I sometimes use reverse perspective.... which leads some people to say 'It didn't look like that to me.'"

This drawing illustrates the interior of the north aisle as it bends around the supports of the northwestern half-dome supporting the west half-dome which in turn supports the great hemisphere over the nave of Hagia Sophia. In other words, if you go into the church from the narthex (entrance hall along the east facade of the building) and turn right, this is what you will see. This is also the only time the text will endeavor to explain one way to look at Catharine's drawings.

Right smack in the middle is a large column on a huge base. It is a superb shaft bound by brass circles to reduce strain. It is of porphyry, a purple granite quarried at only one site in Egypt, a source denied the Byzantines after the Arab invasion of 641-642. Porphyry is purple in color with white specks, which heighten its intense hue. Above the brass band at the neck is a large capital with further architectural elaboration above. Your eye will probably travel up along the inside of the arch supported by the column, then drop down to the vast uncluttered interior of the church, the nave itself. A few figures have been included for scale. Finally your eye may follow around to the left of the column and see another series of spaces along the north aisle. And on the left is a tall figure, way out of scale to the rest of the drawing, but serving as a vertical thrust to the vault above, unnaturally skewered but effective nevertheless in moving the eye to the arch above the porphyry column and down again. The shaft acts as a pivot to all the mad elements swirling about it.

Hagia Sophia, Istanbul, interior, north aisle with view into the nave $\Rightarrow$

8/8/67

Hagia Sophia, Istanbul, interior, and the great northeast hemicycle
with the north aisle beyond the gallery above

$\Rightarrow$

Hagia Sophia, Istanbul, interior, view from south aisle looking north and west

⟹

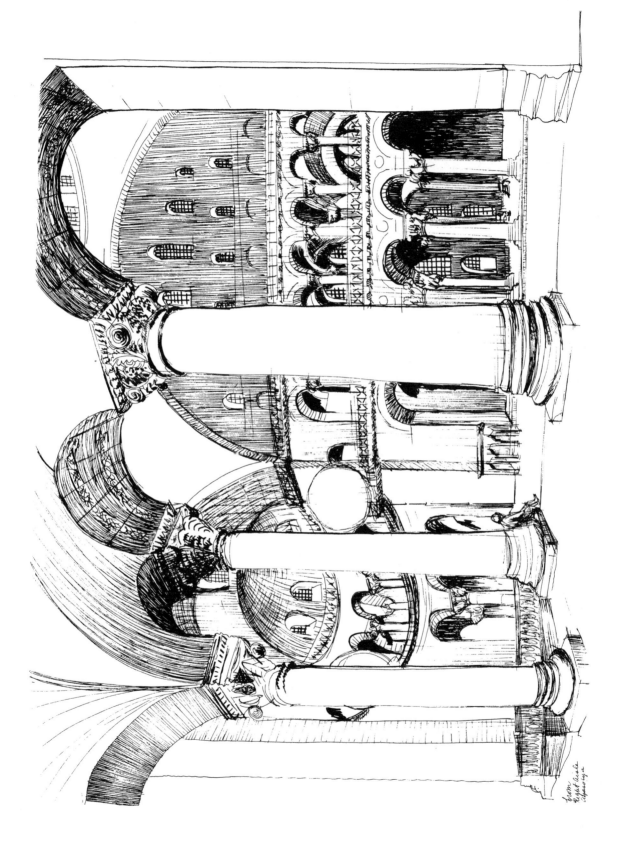

from
Royal Scala
Abu Simbel

Hagia Sophia, Istanbul, interior, south gallery, view of southwest hemicycle looking northwest
$\Rightarrow$

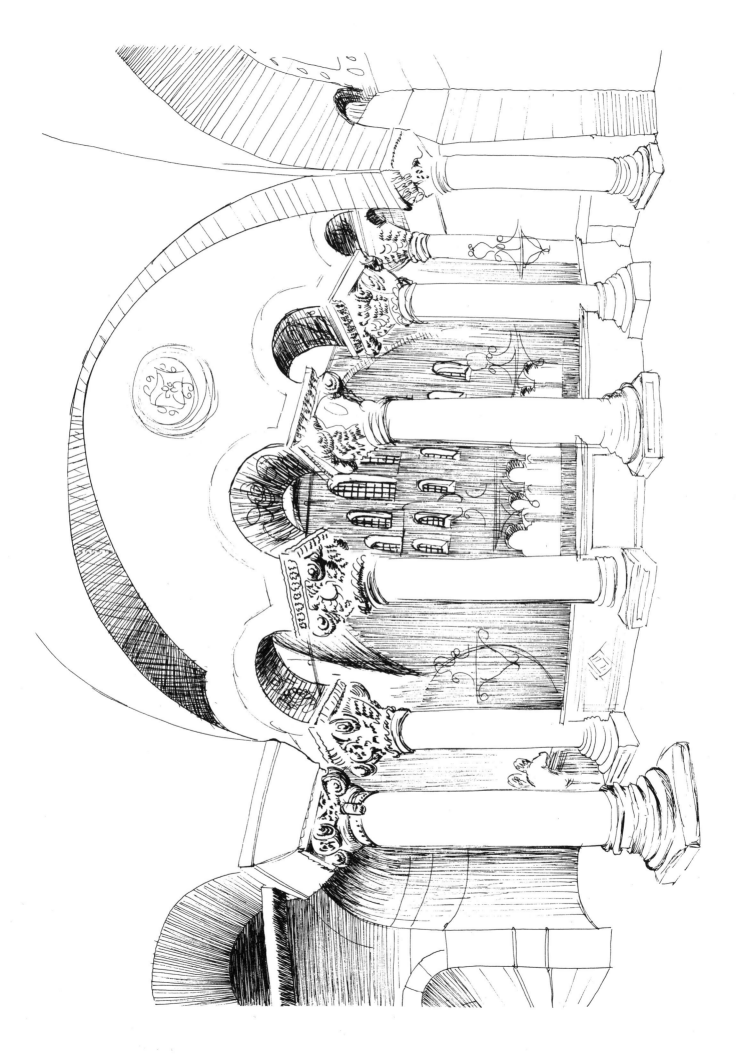

Kücük (Little) Hagia Sophia

(Saints Sergius and Bacchus, Istanbul)

Kücük Hagia Sophia or Ss. Sergius and Bacchus as it was originally dedicated was probably built as a palace chapel for Justinian when he was heir apparent. Theodora, who had the role of a successful Mrs. Simpson to the successor of the throne, was given a special dispensation to marry Justinian, needed because she had been a member of the entertainment class. She, it was, history says, who boldly proclaimed to the Imperial Council that she was an Empress and would die one, on the occasion of the Nike Riots which destroyed almost all public buildings in the capital city. Justinian was ready to flee aboard a navy ship but she held firm while General Belisarius swept the rabble from the streets. Even the basilica of Hagia Sophia had been destroyed. The sovereigns set about rebuilding it immediately to replace the church constructed under Constantine in the fourth century and restored under Theodosius II in the fifth.

Ss. Sergius and Bacchus was apparently unharmed by the fury of the mob. It is called in architectural parlance a central-type building; that is, it has a vertical central axis about which parts are symmetrically disposed, as in the shape of a Greek cross, an octagon or a square. Ss. Sergius and Bacchus is an octagon inscribed within a square. The central space rises three stories and is surrounded by an aisle and gallery, on all but the east. Its decorations are similar to those found later in Hagia Sophia. During Justinian's reign the churches of the capital were covered by mosaics with gold glass backgrounds and floral patterns.... there were no historical figured scenes, for example, in Hagia Sophia until much later. In contrast to the evolution of architecture in the West, the Byzantine world evolved a central type of architecture for worship.

Hagia Sophia is, however, unusual in that it combines a vertical axis (check the drawings) with a horizontal one. The enormous central dome rests on four gigantic piers separated by half-domes, each supported by three smaller half-domes to the east and west. To the north and south there are only sheer window walls above the galleries. This eventually necessitated (a long time later) the addition of massive exterior buttresses.

Saints Sergius and Bacchus, a completely central type of structure with adequate support on each corner for the dome, has remained in rather pristine condition. The floor of the interior has risen considerably because of maintenance and rehabilitation.

Kücük (Little) Hagia Sophia, (Ss. Sergius and Bacchus) Istanbul,
interior view to northeast exedra.

$\Rightarrow$

Kucuk Aya Sofya

S.+B.
6/20/67

Imrahor Cami (St. John Studion)
Istanbul

Imrahor Cami or St. John of the Studion (5th century) is an overgrown ruin. The roof is gone and the walls have decayed in irregular picturesqueness. Typical brick and mortar construction was used and covered by marble revetment. The columns are monoliths of expensive marble and granite. New, it was an impressive establishment and continued to be one of the most richly endowed monasteries of Constantinople. The monks played an important role during the Iconoclastic controversy, a crisis of conscience which occupied political authority for over a hundred years (726-843) focusing on the worthiness of reproducing the divine through matter. Today, the ruins are usually deserted and in the summer resound to the hum of insects.

Imrahor Cami (St. John Studion), Istanbul, nave ruins to the east with the ruins of a Turkish mihrab to the right in the apse.

⇐

Narthex
Imrahor
6/30/67

Imrahor Cami (St. John Studion), Istanbul, interior to west entrance

⇐

Mid-Byzantine Architecture, Istanbul

Bodrum Cami, Istanbul

Two churches among Catharine's drawings represent mid-Byzantine or the Second Golden Age of Byzantine Architecture: the Bodrum Cami, the Church of the Myrelaion Monastery (we do not know its dedication) and Fenari Isa Cami, the Church of Constantine Lips (whose dedication is likewise unknown). The Mid-Byzantine period is traditionally considered to have begun with the reign of Basil the Macedonian, after the forcible removal of his patron, Emperor Michael III, the Drunkard. Basil was a brilliant politician and established an effective, much beloved dynasty that was eventually succeeded by the Comnenian family, equally brilliant administrators, who ruled into the twelfth century.

Mid-Byzantine religious architecture is perfectly suited to the mode of worship that had become established in the Orthodox church. These buildings are not congregational as are the buildings in use in the West. They are small, their interiors dark, and their sanctuaries hidden behind screens to protect the holiness of their rites from profanation. The church itself has become a symbol within which the Christian mystery occurs. The important thing is awareness rather the participation. The building represents the cosmos and is decorated, when possible with mosaics or frescoes depicting sacred history and beings. Architectural forms became set in the mid-Byzantine period. The structures were like jeweled reliquaries. They were completely vaulted with domes and various types of barrel vaults normally constructed of brick and mortar but if available of stone as well. As time went on the ingeniously varied courses of brick, colored stones and tile created interesting textures and polychromed surfaces. The later a Byzantine building the more complex the variations in its walls.

The Bodrum Cami is a complicated structure with an upper church and a lower church used as a mortuary chamber. It seems to have been raised on a platform elevated from its surroundings because it was built over a cistern, part of the water storage so essential to the city.

As with so many of the churches remaining in Istanbul, the Bodrum Cami was built to give evidence of the greatness of an individual through a luxurious monument containing his tomb, in this case Romanos I Lekapenos, who reigned from 920 to 940. In 908, he had dedicated a monastery on the same location to the Mother of God (Theotokos) and the Bodrum Cami was but an addition to the complex. Romanos Lekapenos was an excellent general and politician. He married the young Emperor, Constantine IX Porphyrogenetos, to his daughter, crowned himself co-emperor, and associated his sons with his rule. Constantine was the actual and rightful heir to the throne, having been "born in the purple" chamber of the Sacred Palace, hence his name Porphyrogenetos. He long survived his father and brothers-in-law.

The Bodrum Cami has a central-type plan, a dome is raised on a high drum, a characteristic of this and later Byzantine architecture. It dominates the lower structure, exposed as four barrel vaults abutting the drum. Visible on the exterior is a wall broken regularly with vertical half-round buttresses strategically placed to relieve the thrusts of the interior barrel vaults. The four corners are filled with groin vaults instead of small cupolas.

Bodrum Cami(Church of the Myrelaion Monastery), Istanbul,
view from the southeast

$\Rightarrow$

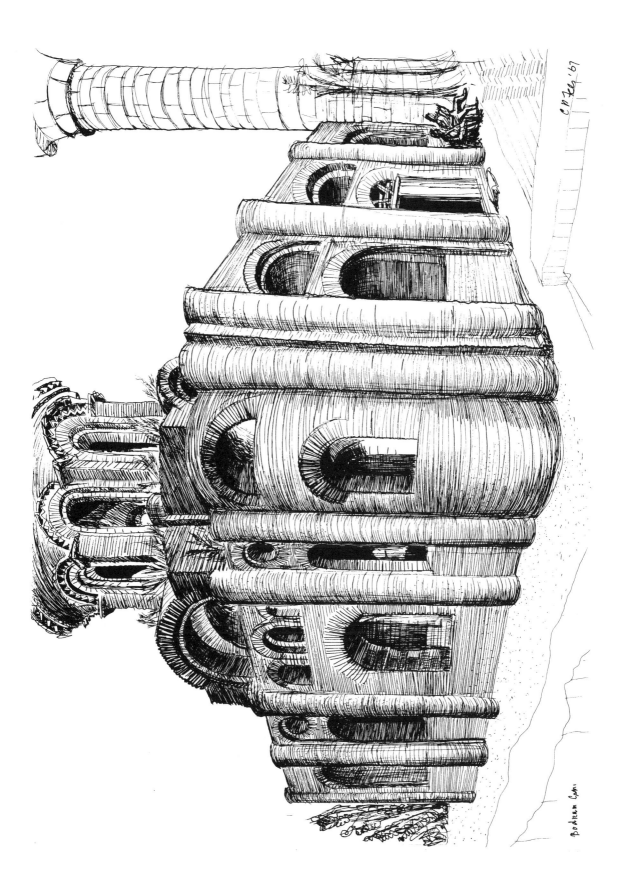

Bodrum Çarşi

CWZe'67

FENARI ISA CAMI (The Church of Constantine Lips), Istanbul

Fenari Isa Cami, founded by Constantine Lips, an admiral of the Byzantine Fleet who was killed in action in 917, has four sections, all of different dates. The north church is the one founded by the Admiral. Next to it to the south is a cruciform area surmounted by a large dome, built during the tenth century. The parekklesion, an added church of one aisle, on the south, was built during the Paleologan period as a mausoleum along with the outer narthex. It dates from the fourteenth century.

Catharine drew it from the rear of the composite building in the narrow space opened behind it. On the right is the oldest and simplest section. In the middle rises the high and typically narrow east end of the mid-Byzantine church. The walls are enhanced by polychromatic brick and stone work. Blind niches on three levels increase the effect of verticality. Next on the left is the parekklesion and last is the closed up end of the exonarthex.

The interior is devoid of all its original decoration except for some exquisite architectural sculpture. In the foreground of the drawing are two column bases whose shafts, along with two others were long ago removed as spoils by the Turks for use in other buildings. Originally the four columns supported the pendentives upon which the dome rested.

Feneri Isa Cami (Church of Constantine Lips), Istanbul, apses from the northeast. Exterior.

$\Rightarrow$

30

Apses
Fenari Isa
Cami

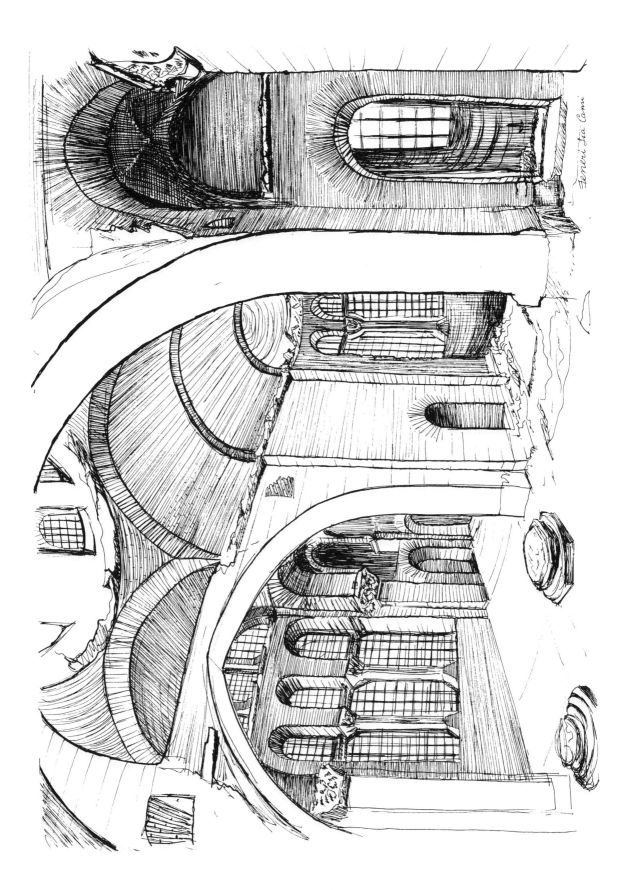

The Third Golden Age of Byzantine Architecture, Istanbul

Fetiye Cami (St. Mary Pammakaristos) and Kariye Cami (Church of the Chora or St. Mary of the Fields)

Two other churches of Istanbul represent the last brilliant period of Byzantine architecture: the parekklesion of Fetiye Cami and the Kariye Cami. The latter, a twelfth century building was remodeled and redecorated in the early fourteenth century at the order of the Grand Logohete, Theodore Metochites, whose portrait with a model of the church appears in the narthex. The church has the good fortune to retain some of the most beautiful mosaics in Istanbul; its parekklesion contains the most superb frescoes. Kariye Cami and Fetiye Cami were both restored by the Dumbarton Oaks Research Library and Collection, Harvard University, as were several other important monuments in Istanbul.

The main church of Kariye Cami consists of two narthexes and a large central room covered by a broad dome on a drum. This dominates, on the exterior, the three domes placed over two bays of the narthex and at the entrance to the parekklesion. The base of an Islamic minaret further unbalances the composition. Quite noticeable is the decorative wall treatment of brick and stone work typical of the period.

Feneri Isa Cami (Church of Constantine Lips), Istanbul, interior from the southwest

⇐

Overleaf: Kariye Cami (Chora or St. Mary of the Fields) Istanbul, from the west

⇒

Kariye Cami (St. Mary of the Fields) parekklesion interior from the west

⇒

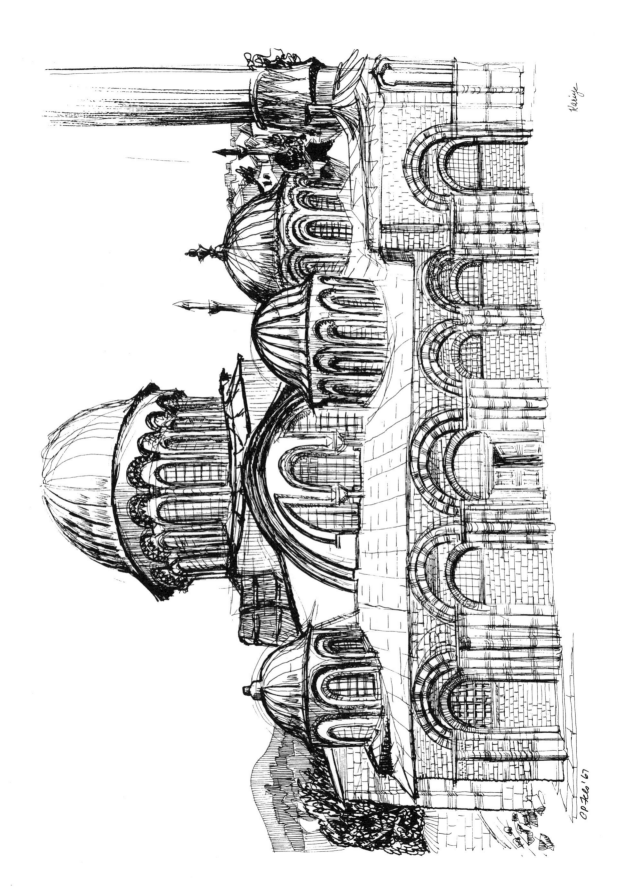

Kariye

OP Feb '67

Kariye Cami
6/23/67
South chapel

Fetiye Cami (St. Mary Pammakaristos)

As its name suggests, the parekklesion of Fetiye Cami belongs to another building. It was constructed as a mausoleum about 1315 in the form of a small, five-spot, quincunx. Its height is about four-and-a-half times its width. It is a little jewel box, almost complete with its original mosaics. It adjoins the church proper, now a functioning mosque. Seen from the exterior, from a small urban garden at the south, the structure is somewhat topheavy because of the overbearing dome of the church in the rear. Nevertheless, the exquisite detailing of the materials of the walls is quite obvious and indicates the high quality of the little chapel-mausoleum within.

Parekklesion of Fetiye Cami (Panagia Pammachristos), Istanbul,
Fetiye Cami in the background, from the southwest

⇒

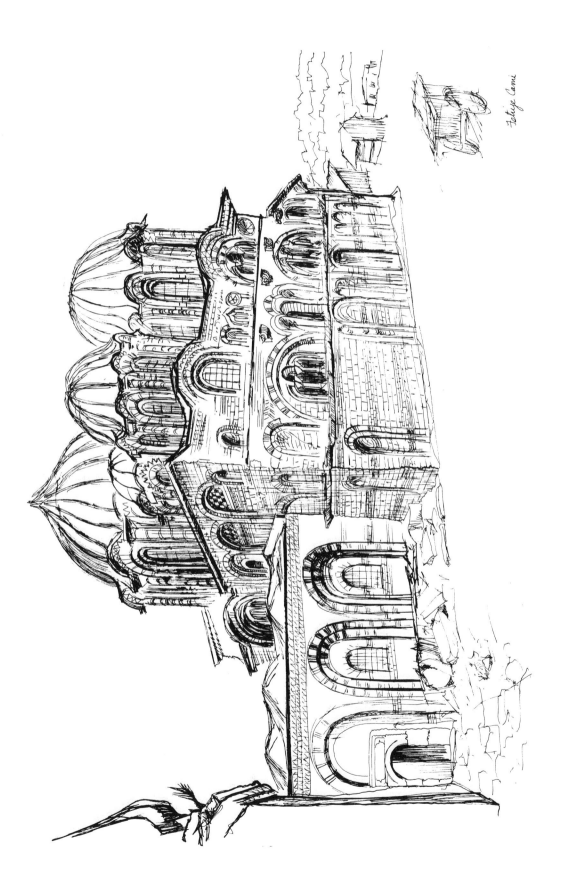

Fatihye Camii

GREECE

Thessalonika

    Thessalonika, or Salonika as it was called, was the second city of the Empire. Thessalonika has always been an important city. It is located at the mouth of a funnel to catch the wealth of the Balkans seeking an outlet to the sea. Although magnificent in terms of its surviving monuments, the city lost an enormous amount of its heritage during the Allied occupation of World War I. What remains is more than impressive and vies with the great cities of antiquity such as Ravenna.

    Surrounded by defensive walls in the fourth century, Thaessalonika was able to withstand attack from Ostrogoths, Visigoths, Huns, Slavs, Avars, Bulgarians, Magyars and others. The city usually remained victorious under the leadership of Saint Demetrios. Some walls still stand on classical foundations, much patched in later times so the walls are like palimpsests of its history. All important Byzantine cities had a girdle of walls. Catharine's drawing of the walls of Ankara clearly show the stratification of repair and addition.

City walls, Thessalonika

⟹

Overleaf: The Citadel Walls of Ankara

⟹

City walk
Thessaloniki

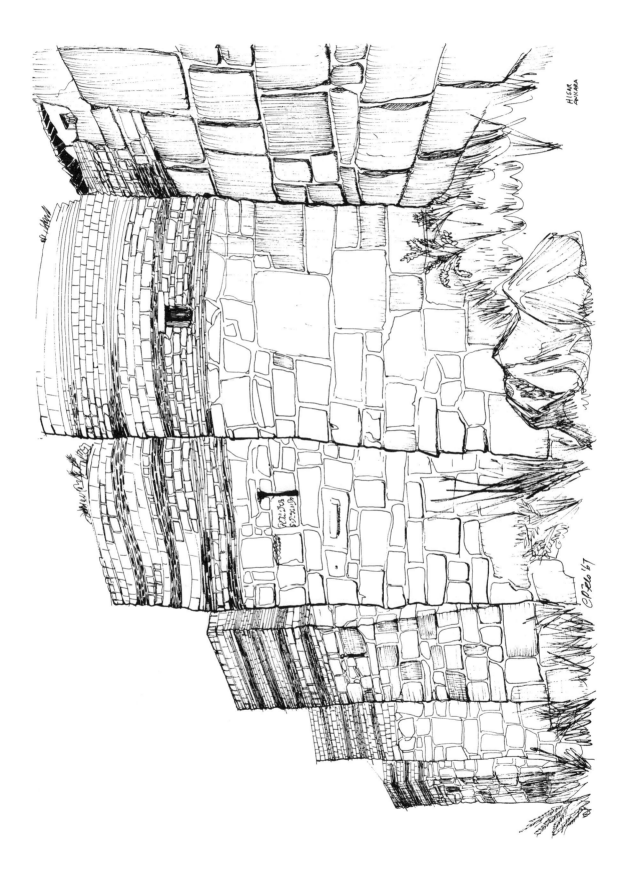

Panaghia Ca
Thessaloniki

Panaghia Chalkeon, Thessalonika

The Panaghia Chalkeon, Our Lady of the Braziers, so called, probably, because it stood in the quarter where copper was manufactured into utensils, was built during the second quarter of the twelfth century. The major feature is the large dome on a two-story drum. Two cupolas were added over the narthex, otherwise the roof lines tend to be angular. The effect is rather blocky but the building has an unusual quality of boldness or strength. Its interior has retained a great deal of its original fresco decoration.

Hagios Apostoli, Thessalonika

The Church of the Holy Apostles belongs to the third Byzantine period. The undulations, proliferations of cupolas with their segmented roofs, curved roof lines, arches and round-headed niches create a visual feast of high sophistication enhanced by the decorative brickwork. The structure reflects the latest developments in Constantinople and should recall, for example, the parekklesion of the Fetiye Cami. The Patriarch of Constantinople, Niphon I, had it built between 1312 and 1315. It has a Greek cross plan with a large narthex wrapped around it.

Panagia Chalkeon, Thessalonika, from the east

$\Longleftarrow$

Hagios Apostoli, Thessalonika, from the southeast

$\Longrightarrow$

42

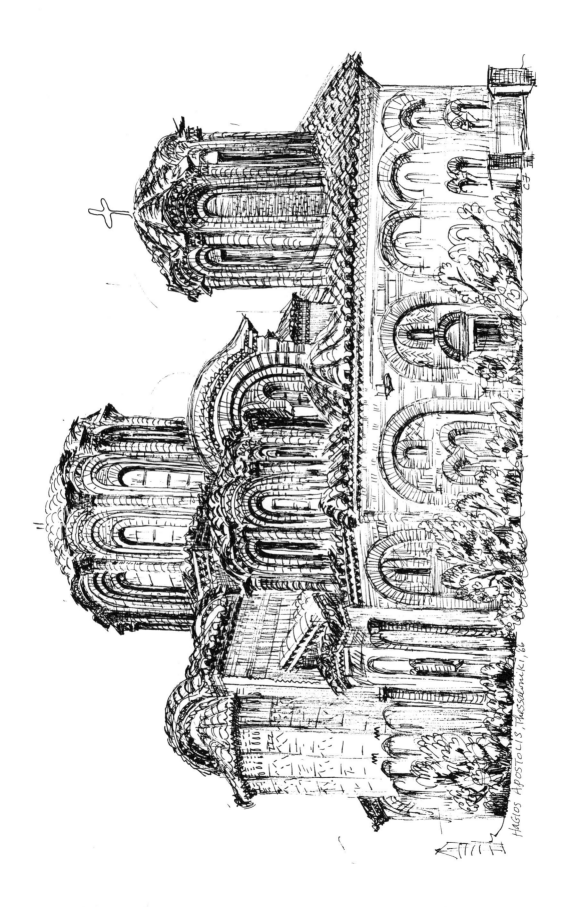

HAGIOS APOSTOLIS, THESSALONIKI, '66

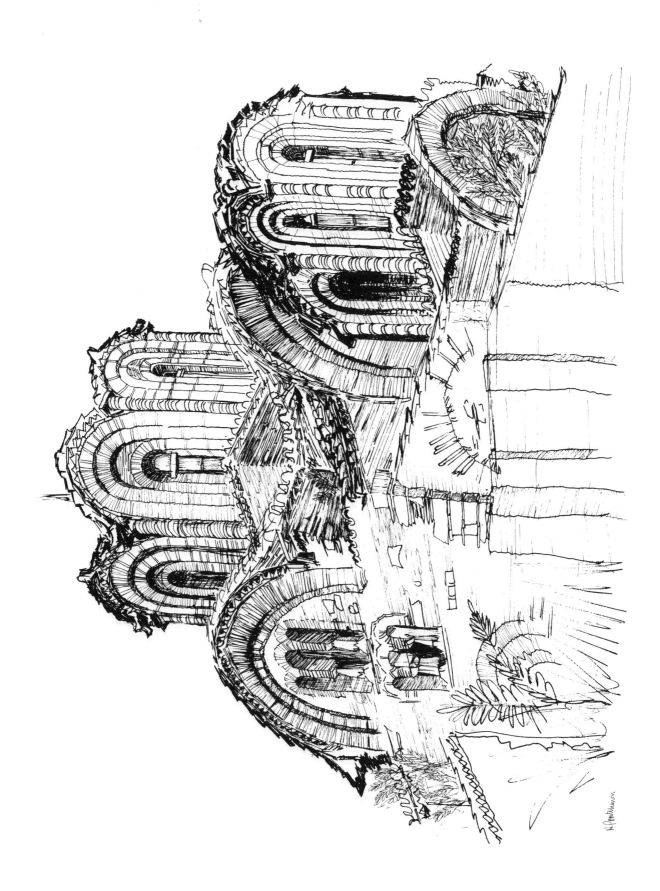

Hagios Panteleimon, Thessalonika, from the northwest
⇐

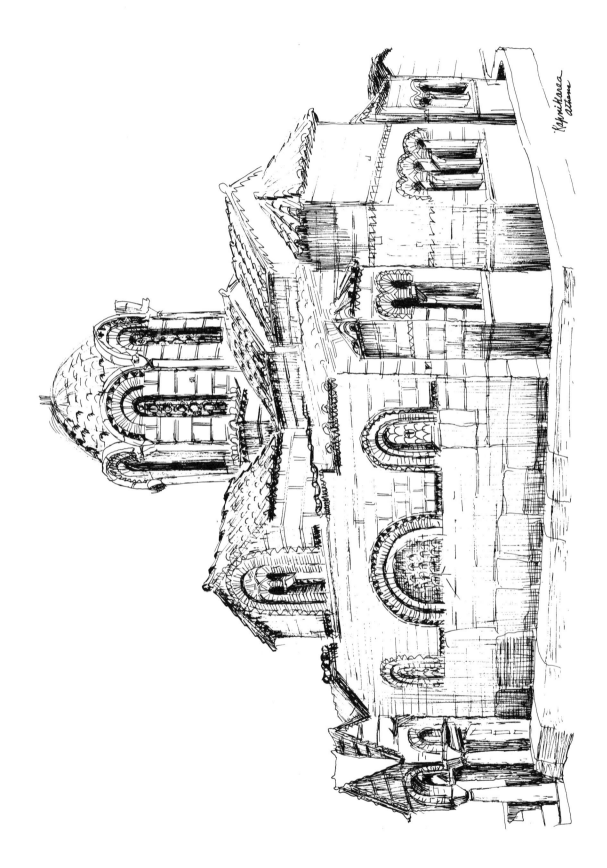

ATHENS

During most of the Middle Ages, Athens was an unimportant provincial town. Its brilliant past conflicted with the Christian present. Further, Greece had been invaded and settled by Slavic peoples, and thus escaped Byzantine hegemony for some three hundred years. The architecture shows this history and the earliest examples are from the eleventh century. In Athens itself, the churches, while charming, are small and rather undistinguished. Only the monastic foundations outside the town achieved great distinction. Among them is the Monastery of Daphne whose mosaic decorations are so superb one is tempted to see it as commissioned from the capital itself.

Church of the Kapnikarea

The little church of the Presentation of the Virgin, the Kapnikarea, is an eleventh-century survivor in the middle of a main thoroughfare. It is a cruciform church; a lateral nave was added to the north, dedicated to Saint Barbara and opened to the older building. Across both of them stretches a narthex. The structure is very dark, peopled by specters and lighted by only a few votive candles. The exterior is charming and throngs of shoppers break to either side of it like waves rushing to shore.

Church of the Kapnikarea, Athens, view from the southeast

⇐

The Little Metropolitan Church

The Little Metropolitan Church, dedicated to Panagia Gorgeopikoos and Hagios Eleftherios, is unique in Greece. It is minuscule and made to seem even more so by its relation to the modern Greek Orthodox Cathedral next to it. The little church is covered with marble slabs taken from every period preceding the twelfth, when it was built; Classical Greek, Roman, Early Christian, and contemporary Byzantine, carved spoils from the past. It is in the form of a Greek cross with a small dome on a drum.

Gabled roofs project to form the base of the drum. The whole is tiled in red.

Little Metropolitan Church, Athens, from the southwest

$\Rightarrow$

48

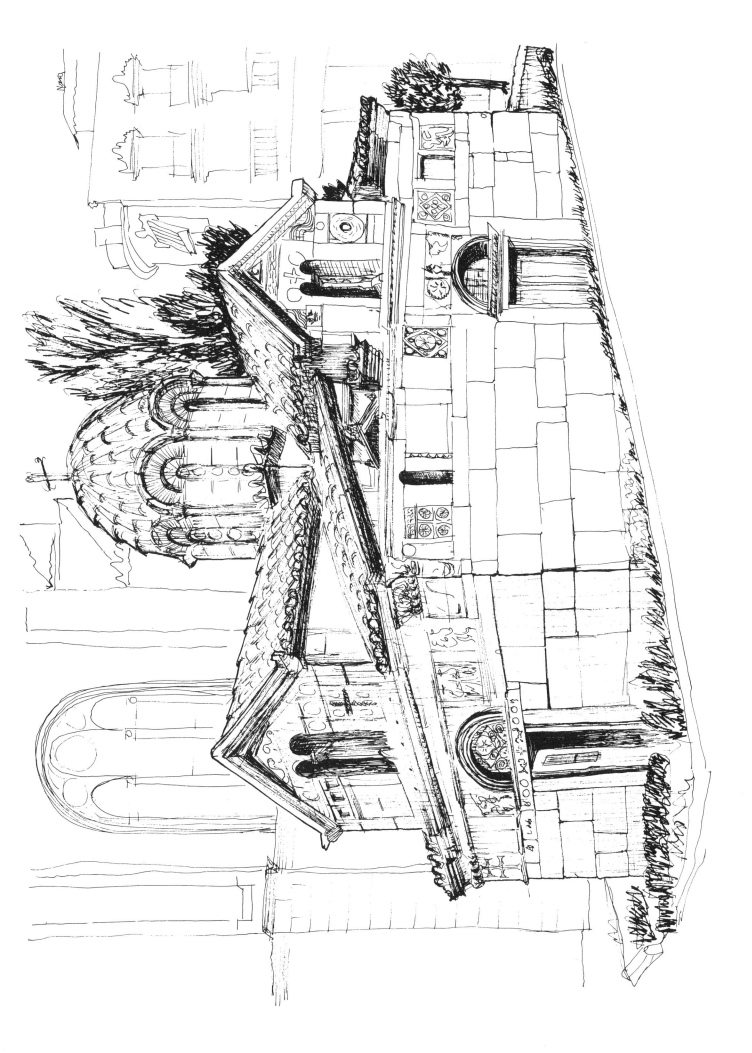

Church of the Metamorphosis (Transfiguration)

Athens ceased to be Byzantine in 1204. Hence the buildings of the Third Golden Age are conservative, though still charming as is the small church of the Transfiguration (Metamorphosis) below the slopes of the Acropolis, underneath the Erectheum and above the Roman Forum. It is extremely picturesque and evocative of all the romance ancient and medieval Greece can juxtapose.

Church of the Metamorphoses (Transfiguration), Athens

⇒

50

METAMORPHOSIS
ATHENS

The Monastery of Daphne

The Monastery of Daphne is now within the urban area of Athens, but was until recently in the country on the way to Megara, located among olive groves. By type, it belongs to the eleventh century, as do its mosaics. There are no records to tell us the history of the structure. Its interior holds a tall central space abutted by barrel vaults and squinches supporting the drum of a flat dome. A narthex was added to the west. Classical Ionic columns were used in its composition. It is very un-Byzantine; in fact, it was constructed for the Latin monks who possessed the monastery after the takeover of Greece by the adventurers of the Fourth Crusade.

In Athens, which gave its name to the Duchy, although the capital was at Thebes, the French were in control after 1204. In 1311 came the Catalan Company, hired at first as a group of mercenaries by the Greek Emperor of Constantinople. They were ultimately succeeded by the Navarrese Company which in turn was replaced by a Florentine family, the Acciauoli, who stayed until the Turks took over in the latter part of the fifteenth century.

Monastery of Daphne, environs of Athens, narthex

$\Rightarrow$

Overleaf: Monastery of Daphne, interior

$\Rightarrow$

Daphni

Dafni.

Virgin Theotokos
at Hosios Loukas

Arsén Lukas

Hoseas Loukas, Phocis

A second great collection of eleventh century mosaics is found at Hoseas Loukas, Stiris, Phocis, not far from Delphi. The quality of the mosaics is not so high as that of Daphne but in completeness they make up for any loss. St. Luke, in this case, was a local hermit saint who retired to this location in the wilds. Two churches of the eleventh century were built on this site, overlooking vast sweeps of unforested land; one, sometimes called the Katholikon, is dedicated to the saint himself, the other to Mary, the Mother of God (Theotokos). The mosaics are in the former and cover not only the narthex but the aisles, galleries and vaults.

Overleaf: Church of the Theotokos, Hosios Loukas, narthex

⇐

Monastery of Hosios Loukas, interior of the Katholikon

⇐

THE PRINCIPALITY OF THE MOREA

Andravida was the capital of the Latin Principality of the Morea from 1204 until 1447, when it was taken by the Byzantines. They lost it to the Turks three years later. The eastern apse, flanked by side chapels, of the Cathedral of Hagia Sophia, is all that remains of the Frankish building of that period in Andravida. The apse is rib-vaulted in Gothic construction. Restoration has not preserved the original style in detail. Ashlar stones taken from nearby classical sites were used in contrast to the brick and tile of Byzantine buildings. The Crusaders found it more expedient to use stone already cut. It is thus a unique relic in Greece. There are two other monuments which retain ribbed vaults but they were attached by the Franks to older buildings. The most delightful is the Church of Our Lady of Vlachernae not far from Andravida, in the northwest tip of the Peloponnesos.

Cathedral of Hagia Sophia, Andravida, Peloponnesos, ruins of sanctuary

⇐

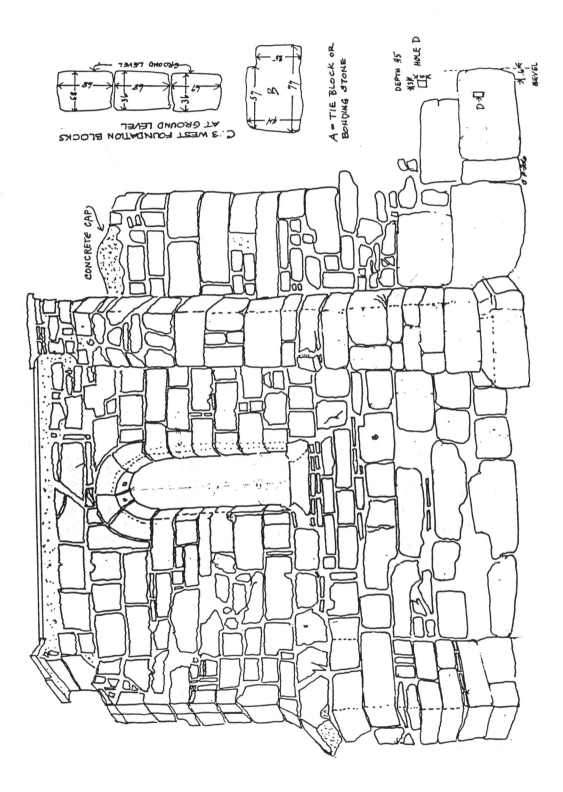

CONCRETE CAP

GROUND LEVEL

87 | 69 | 67

35 | 31 | 31

C.3 WEST FOUNDATION BLOCKS
AT GROUND LEVEL

58

57 | B | 77

44

A = TIE BLOCK OR
BONDING STONE

DEPTH 95

HOLE D

D

BEVEL

Cathedral of Hagia Sophia, Andravida

"My experience of the Hagia Sophia, Andravida, was quite different from my experience of other medieval buildings in Eastern Europe. I was much better acquainted with it than any other building except Hagia Sophia, Istanbul. What was unique in my experience of Hagia Sophia, Andravida, was not so much the ruin itself as the town and the surrounding countryside, the other Crusader ruins nearby. I was sure that I saw many stones from Hagia Sophia built into buildings in Andravida itself. Perhaps there were some in the little building we rented for an office. These stones were easy to identify, I thought, by the amount of wear, the color of the stones, and the presence of clamp holes used in classical construction.

"The most interesting and also the nearest to Andravida of the other Crusader buildings is Chlemoutzi. It crowns the top of a hill between Killini Port and Killini Loutra and is visible for many miles, though not from the ruin at Andravida. It is a huge structure with a keep, extensive walls, housing for men and horses, a portcullis gate--the whole medieval castle organization. It was very hard to draw because of its great size. If I got close enough to see any detail I couldn't see the whole thing. The best view of it was from the trash dump of Kastro, the village on the slopes below the castle. I tried once to work there but found it impossible to stay because of the flies."

Hagia Sofia, Andravida, north wall,
north chapel, not drawn to scale

$\Leftarrow$

Overleaf: Castle of Chlemoutzi, view from the southeast

$\Rightarrow$

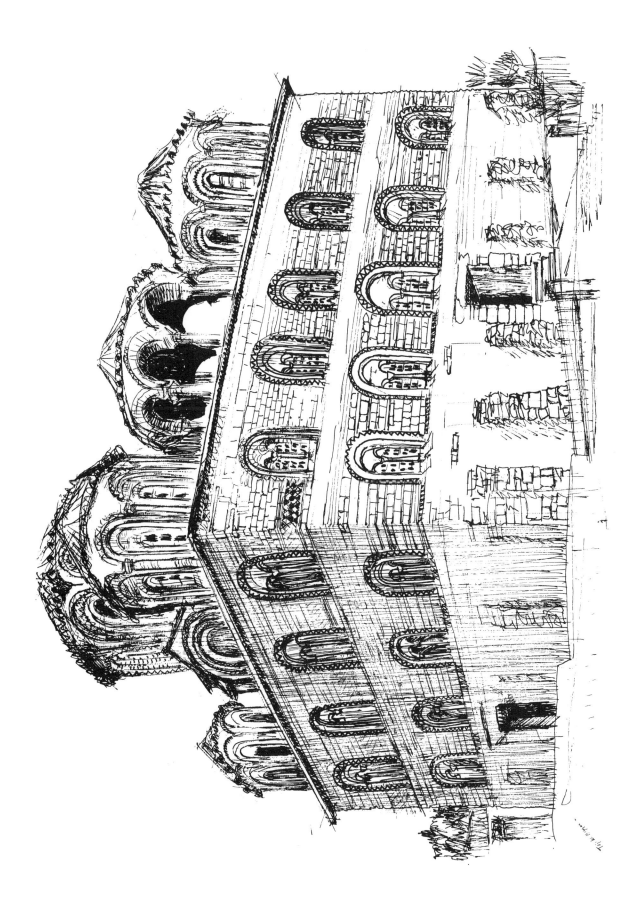

Panaghia Perigoritissa
Arta 7/29/66

The Despotate of Arta

Andravida is unique in Greece; so also are the medieval buildings of Arta, capital of the Epirus. Although Byzantine in nature they show an inventiveness not present elsewhere in the Byzantine cultural region. After the debacle of the Fourth Crusade and the loss of Constantinople, the Greeks rallied at the extremes of the former Empire: Trebizond and Arta, and at Nicaea as well. Members of the Paleologue family became the Despots of the Epirus, fought for dominance against the other heirs of Constantinople, and allied themselves with the Franks of the Morea and the Angevin French of Naples.

The Despots were responsible for most of the churches to be seen at Arta. Anna Paleologue was the patronness of the Cathedral, the Panaghia Perigoritissa, or Our Lady of Consolation. It gives an impression of a great box because the narthex is carried two stories high; its walls rise sheer to a heavy modern overhang. The gallery above the narthex certainly served the royal house as a place for worship with access directly from the palace, a traditional disposition since late antiquity. The interior is equally startling because of the supports for the squinches below the dome. Instead of piers, as at Daphne, or four columns, as at Fenari Isa, the architect corbelled sections of column shafts into the walls as support for columns placed vertically for two stories in the central space and three for a facing to the sanctuary. The result, now, with the structure stripped bare of most of its covering, is awkward, blocky and bulky, but seen with its original mosaics and sculptures it must have been exciting and impressive.

Overleaf: Panagia Perigoritissa, Arta, seen from northwest

⇐

Panagia Perigoritissa, Our Lady of Consolation, the Cathedral of Arta, interior to the sanctuary

⇐

Hagios Basilios, Arta, view from the northeast, showing decorative and cloisonne-brick and tile work. The building is a three-aisled basilica. Note also how the wall over the apse juts up over the roof and stands free.

⇒

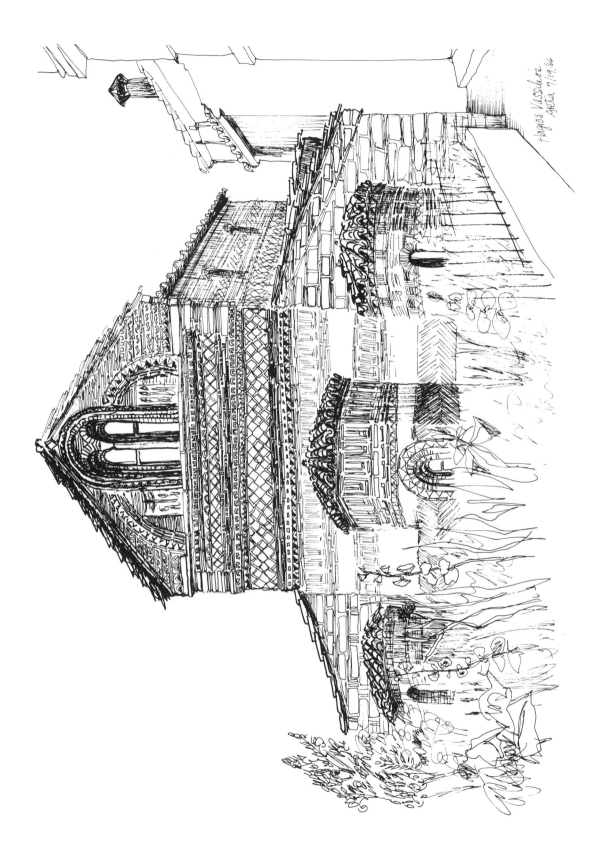

Hagia Vassilios
Syros 7/19/66

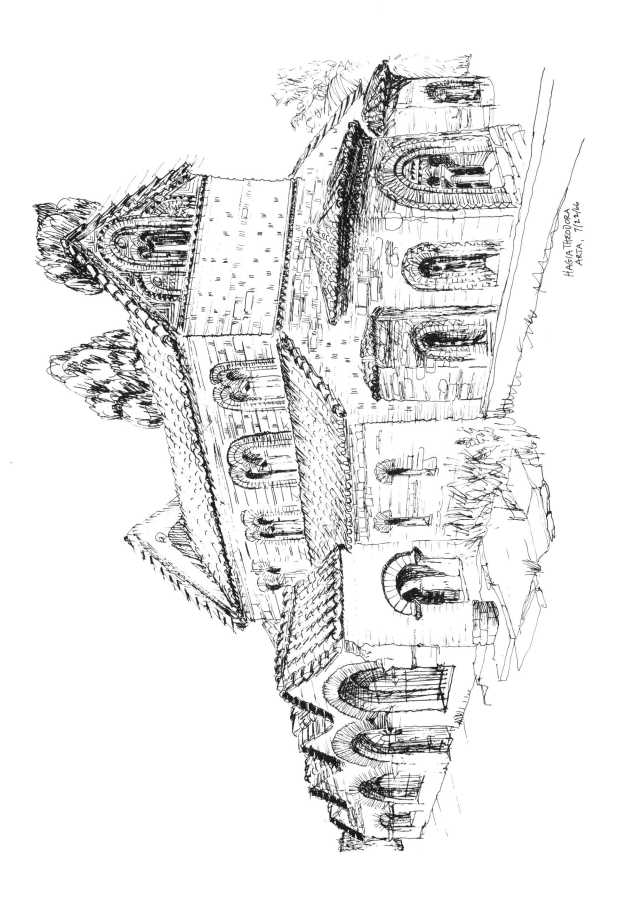

HAGIA THEODORA
ARTA, 7/22/66

METEORA - MONI ROUSSANO

THE MONASTERIES OF THE METEORA

The Meteora is an agglomeration of separate monasteries built as the name implies "in the air." Geological differential erosion has made the region an extraordinary vision of decayed mountains, precipices, crags, rocks.... a violent natural upheaval. When they were built, the monasteries achieved as nearly perfect protection as was provided in Medieval Greece. The establishments date to the Third Byzantine Golden Age and are typical of the architecture of the period. Hundreds of feet in the air, the buildings soar over thin needles of stone, seemingly about to tumble into deep abysses. The area near Kalabaka is one of the most romantic and picturesque of Europe. Several other sites have a similar eroded landscape used by man for habitation, worship and protection. The best known and most visited sites are Guadix in Spain and Göreme in Anatolia.

Overleaf: Hagia Theodora, Arta, view from the northeast, a three aisled basilica

⇐

Moni Russano, Meteora

⇐

Overleaf: Hagia Triada, Meteora

⇒

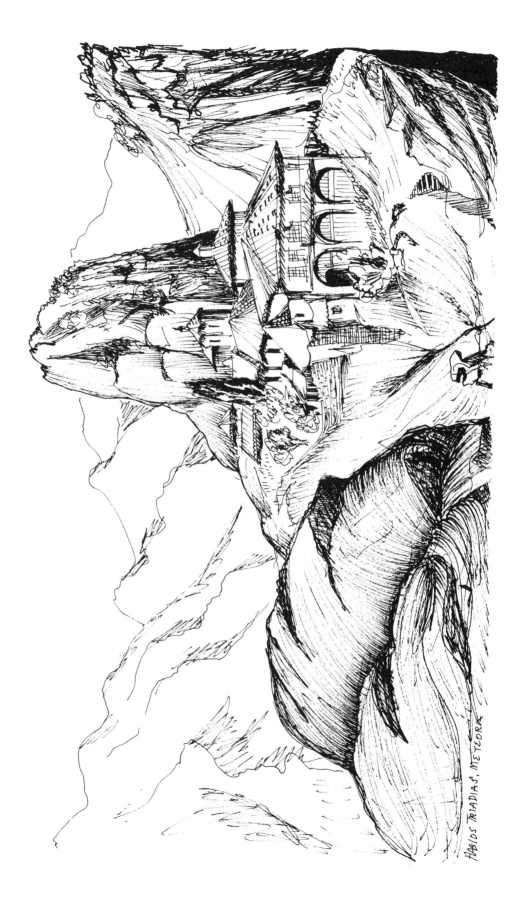

HAGIOS TRIADIAS, METEORA

LASCARIS HOUSE

Mistra is more than an assemblage of buildings. It is a whole city, surrounded by walls and topped by an impregnable citadel. In the Middle Ages, it replaced classical Sparta, which had come to be known as Lacedaemonia. This city was abandoned for the security offered by Mistra's castle in 1264. As things go in the Balkans, Mistra is fairly recent, but its ruins are among the most evocative. The city was abandoned because of earthquake damage. Its history and location are so unusual that even Goethe wrote about it in the second act of Faust. Many of its churches remain, as do the paved pathways up and around its hill. But almost everything else is gone, except for the palace of the rulers.

The story of Mistra is linked to that of Andravida, the capital of the Franks of the Principality of the Morea. The de Villhardouin family had established itself throughout the Peloponnese except for the extreme southeasterly portion as a result of the Fourth Crusade. In 1249, Guillamme de Villehardouin, the second prince of the dynasty, conquered even that area and established near Lacdaemonia a fortification on top of a hill which sweeps steeply to a crest and falls sharply down. Curtain walls of the fort still crown the heights of Mistra. The fort clings to the sloping sides of the mount and is surrounded by walls. In case of peril, the townspeople below could find security within the confines of the open construction along the top of the ridge.

For his third wife, Guillamme, who was to have no descendants, married Anna, a daughter of the Despot of Arta, Michael II Angelus. The Franks of the Peloponnese and those of the Kingdom of Sicily allied themselves with Arta and engaged in war with the ambitious Greek Emperor of Constantinople, founder of the Byzantine Third golden Age, Michael VIII Paleologus. During the crucial battle for the Epirus, Michael Angelus pulled his troops out. The Emperor Michael captured all the barons of the Principality of the Morea and demanded ransom for their release.

Three years later the men returned to Andravida, thanks to the decisions of their wives, who then controlled the baronies. Mistra and two other fortifications were sacrificed to Constantinople as partial payment of the ransom. From 1262, Mistra was Greek again. Her territory expanded at the expense of the Franks until it included the entire peninsula. Mistra became the second city of the dying Empire, displaying great creative energy and political acumen.

House of Lascaris

It is somewhat confusing and difficult to separate the secular buildings in Catharine's drawing of the house of the Lascaris family. At its base is a large arch, opening into a barrel vaulted hall with rooms above which have arched windows. This was a typical house at Mistra, and is the best preserved. Utility space below, living quarters above make this a characteristic Mediterranean house. Here the material is stone and the interiors are vaulted; openings are arched. Behind the house are other walls and buildings; above all rises the Church of the Pantanassa.

⇐   House of Lascaris, Mistra

Convent of the Pantanassa, Mistra, seen from the east   ⇒

Church of the Virgin Pantanassa

Climbing uphill, Catharine staked out a place for her chair and sketch pad, and drew the Church of the Virgin (Pantanassa) from a typical sharp angle. The Pantanassa was consecrated in 1428 and is one of the last churches to be erected while Mistra was still free from the Turks. It displays the inventiveness of the Mistra school in its combination of longitudinal and central plan, along with a free-standing bell tower in its upper stories. Otherwise the typical late Byzantine vocabulary of decoration and form is present. Further influences, resulting in the appearance of relief sculptures, indicate the receptive and innovative spirit present at Mistra.

The ground floor of the Pantanassa has a broad nave and side aisles. The gallery, however, wraps around three sides of a central section which opens to a dome whose diameter is that of the width of the nave below. The arrangement translates space in a startling way from a directional path to a vertical thrust upward to the heavens. It is the only active church at Mistra and is occupied by a convent of nuns.

Convent of the Pantanassa, Mistra, interior of the gallery

⇒

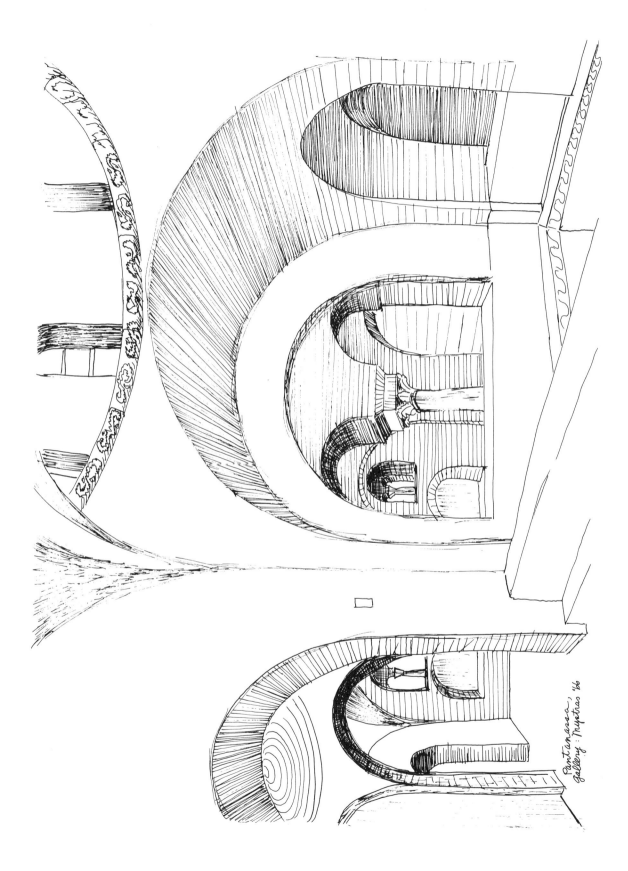

Pantanaaa,
Gallery: Tryptuo '86

Church of the Virgin Peribleptos

The Church of the Virgin Peribleptos has a great charm as it huddles against the hill and descends the terrain in steps which open to interior staircases. In contrast to the Pantanassa, this church is of a purely central type, a cross inscribed within a square with the requisite domes above. Its bell tower sits well above and away from the building. The glory of the Peribleptos is in its frescoes. These rank with contemporary fourteenth century Italian creations of such well-known artists as Duccio de Buonisegna. The unknown artists at Mistra and Duccio both succeed in softening Byzantine formulae and point the way to the ever-increasing humanization of art which culminated in the fifteenth century Italian Renaissance movement.

Church of the Afendiko (Odigitria)

The largest open space still extant in the city belongs to the Brontochion Monastery with its two churches, the Afendiko (Odigitria) and Theordorii. The double storied narthex of the Afendiko is open to the plains below, the church itself is of the same type as the Pantanassa, a broad nave with aisles and a gallery above, treated as a five-spot domed structure. The church with its court now serves as the Museum of Mistra.

Mistra became so important, militarily and economically, to the Byzantine Empire that the sovereigns of the time appointed their heirs as the Despots of the territory. Constantinople fell to the Turks in 1453. Mistra survived until 1460. She was well treated by the conquering Turks and was destroyed, as mentioned above, by earthquakes, not by war.

Church of the Peribleptos, Mistra, view from the east

⟹

Overleaf: Church of the Afendiko, Mistra, Narthex Court

⟹

PERIVLIPTOS
Mystras '66

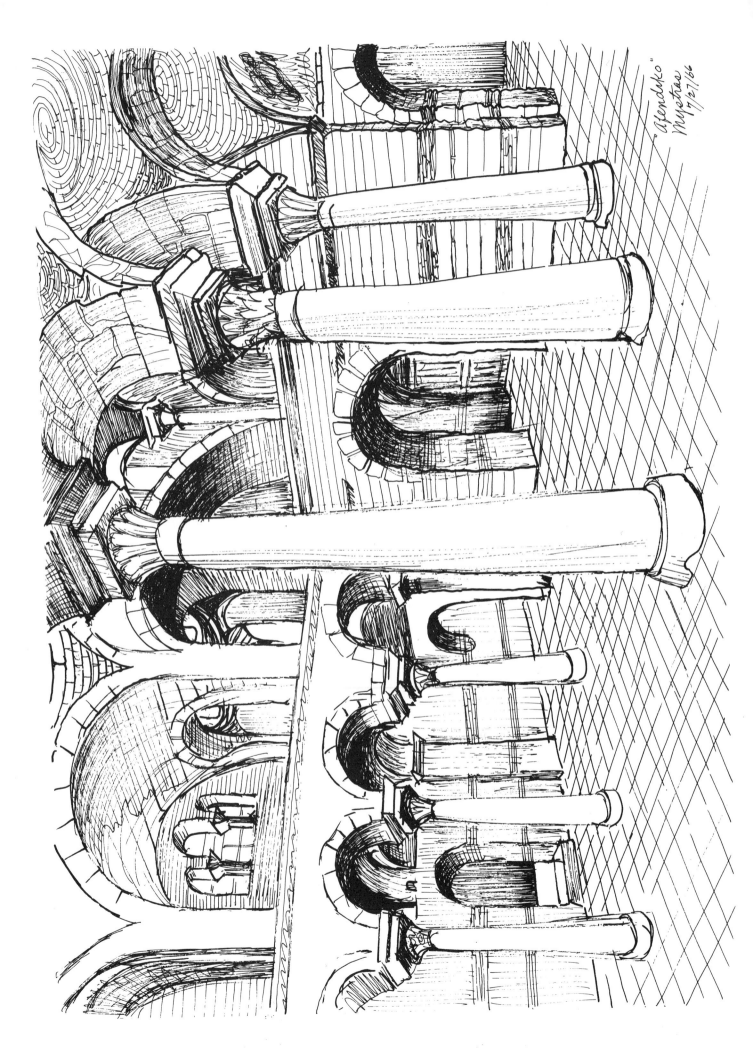

YUGOSLAVIA

Modern Yugoslavia, which came into being after World War I, groups together nations of great cultural diversity. The modern split between church allegiance to the Vatican and to the Eastern Orthodox community is part of this diversity. The division between the coastal and the interior regions dates back to the establishment of the provinces of the Roman Empire. Culturally, Dalmatia (Croatia and Slovenia) is "western." The interior, in fact the rest of the Balkans, is "eastern." Catharine drew her way through the regions whose barbaric invaders of the fifth, sixth and seventh centuries were civilized by Byzantium. Byzantine culture, particularly the religion, was developed, copied, aped from the seventh to the fifteenth century, and thereafter Turkish Istanbul still exerted the pull of a great focal metropolis.

The ebb and flow of Byzantine political hegemony resulted in the diffusion of the religious arts of Constantinople: architecture and mural decoration, the minor arts, indeed all the baggage of Byzantium. This culture and its changing aspects were abetted by the local Bulgarian rulers, the Asens, or by the Namanja family of the Serbians. Specific but more ephemeral rulers and high church officials were also responsible for the creation of fascinating monuments in the region.

A Street Leading from the Central Thoroughfare up to the Walls, Dubrovnik

⇐

The Walls of Kotor   ⇒

Two drawings graphically present the ruggedness of the terrain of much of western Serbia and of Macedonia and the type of urban spaces and walled protection required even in that rugged terrain. Neither Kotor nor Dubrovnik, old Ragusa, belonged to the Byzantine cultural orbit in spite of being dependent on its navy for maritime protection along the Adriatic; each partakes of the inhospitable Yugoslav terrain. The walls of Kotor do go up vertically with enormous rapidity. Within such protective ramparts were and are streets that rise steeply and are interrupted by steps like the picturesque path at Dubrovnik as it winds its wearing but romantic way.

Kotor has one of the most extraordinary situations in the world. From the Adriatic one enters a fiord that soon branches into two forks. Along the southern waterway to the east, against a precipitous mountain, lies the town. Secure in its water bastion, Kotor prospered during the Middle Ages and later as a lair for pirates. So famous was Kotor that Peter the Great of Russia sent his naval cadets there for training.

Catharine says, "The Bay of Kotor is one of my favorite places. There steep gray karst mountains plunge down to the water. Here and there a green valley reaches back into mountain hideaways. Trees seem to grow on rooftops, long grass hangs out of windows. A severe earthquake had damaged the town badly before my 1980 visit. The dark narrow streets, old palaces, cathedral square, but most of all the steep slopes behind the town make Kotar unusually picturesque, even on that dramatic coast.

"A Renaissance town hall is used as a factory, the hum of many sewing machines startled us as we waited for a bus to back and turn its bulk at the dockside.

"On both trips, we were repeatedly warned of the difficulty of the road between Titograd (the capital of Montenegro and upcountry from Kotor) and Pec. It's a narrow winding road, surfaced in 1980. To an American westerner, it doesn't seem too difficult. One can see approaching traffic from quite a distance and pull off at a wide spot."

Sveti Sophia, Ochrid, view from the north $\Rightarrow$

OCHRID

Inland from Kotor, over the mountains and a bit to the south, lies the Lake of Ochrid and the town of the same name. Throughout the Middle Ages, the Via Egnatia ran to Ochrid from the coastal city of Dyrachium, now in modern Albania, on its way to Thessalonika and Constantinople. It was the Roman road linking the old Italian capital to the new one on the Golden Horn.

Relatively secure in its isolation behind the coastal mountains to the west and to the south by the tortuous mountains down the Vardar River Valley, Ochrid flourished and for a time was even the head of a political entity. Ochrid retains a prestigious number of Byzantine buildings. The old town rises on sharp hills and looks south and east to Sveti Naum, the unbelievably beautiful location of a Byzantine church. Perhaps because Ochrid looks westward to the forbidden shores of Albania or just because of the beauty of the locale, it is one of the splendid and intriguing sites of the Balkans.

Sveta Sophia, Ochrid

The Church of Sveta Sophia at Ochrid, as the name suggests served as the principle ecclesiastic structure of Ochrid and may date back to the ninth century. It may have been reconstructed in the eleventh century, as well as later, and is again under restoration. The design is heavy and solid with a nave and aisles and a two-storied porch across the facade. The building is therefore atypical of much of the architecture of Constantinople but serves as an example of variations that occur even in the rather strict code of Byzantine architecture.

Sveti Naum, Lake Ochrid

The church of Sveti Naum is a little gem set near the springs that feed Lake Ochrid. "The church is a favorite pilgrimage place for Yugoslavs who revere Sveti Naum because he was one of the first pupils of Cyril and Methodius who developed the Cyrilic alphabet, which is still used in Serbia.

"A boat goes from Ochrid daily in summer to the south end of the lake which borders on Albania. The fence that divides Yugoslavia and Albania is almost at the edge of the Sventi Naum churchyard. We were seriously warned not to be tempted to cross the fence by United States citizens visiting their homeland. U.S. citizens cannot go to Albania, though Albanians and Yugoslavs go back and forth.

"The peacocks that stroll around the little building and on its roof add to its charm. The springs that feed the lake rise in great crystal pools near the church. I can't help noting that the locations of such springs are holy places all over the near east."

Sveti Naum, Church, from the northwest $\Rightarrow$

84

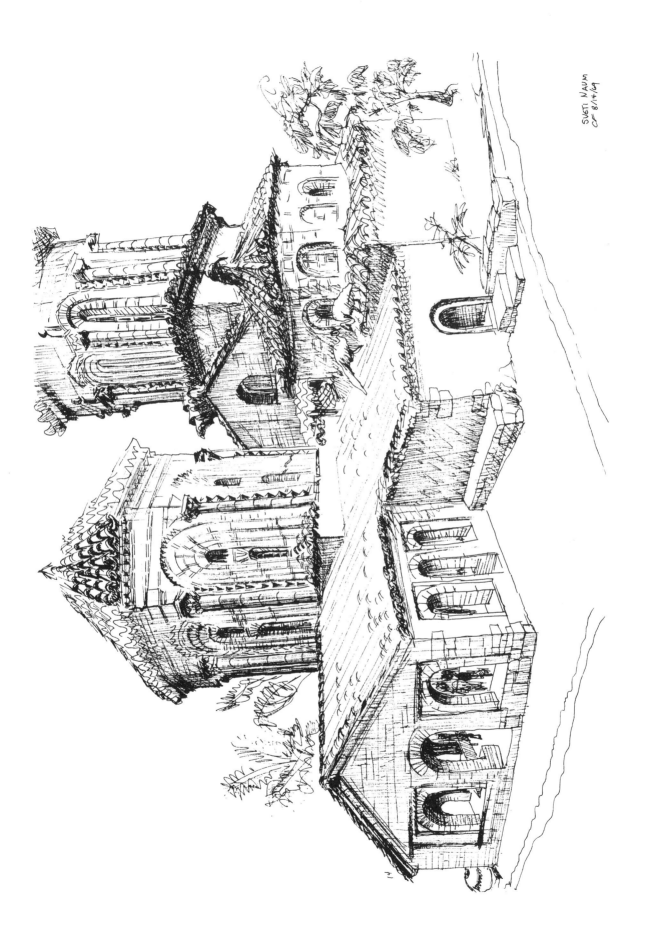

SVETI NAUM
CF 8/14/09

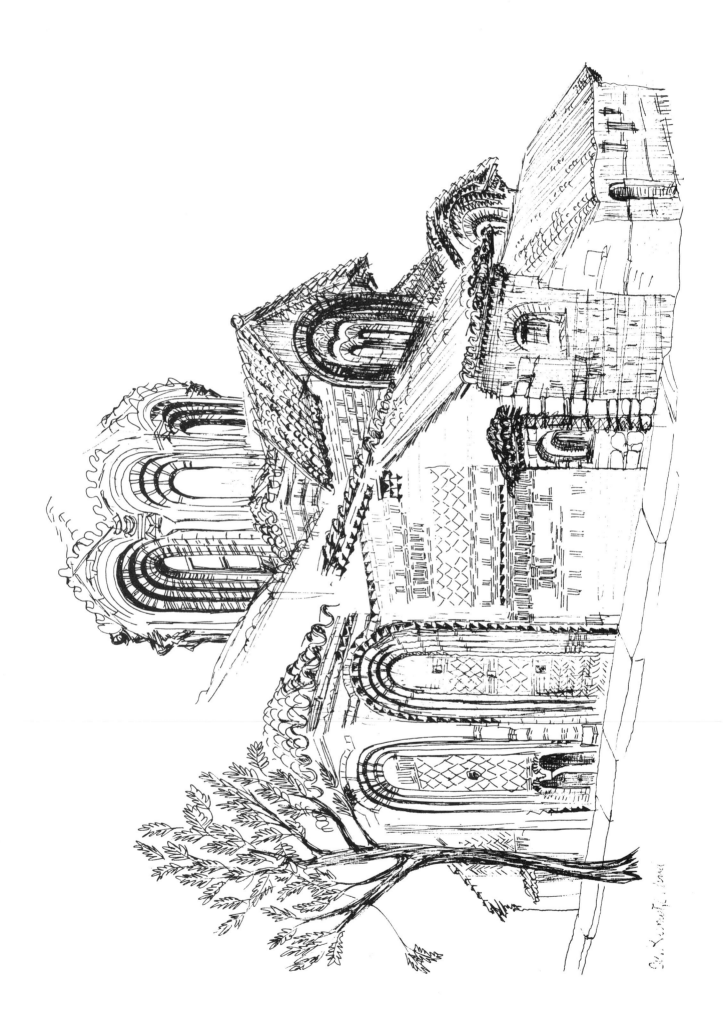

Sveti Panteleimon, Nerezi

"The twelfth century Church of Sveti Panteleimon at Nerezi sits on a wooded hillside west of Skopje. The day we visited, Tito was there to dedicate it as a national monument.... part of a celebration of the fiftieth anniversary of the day Turkey ceded Macedonia to Yugoslavia and Greece.

"Sveti Panteleimon at Nerezi is a sturdy building with a large central tower and four corner towers, squared apses, one large and the other ones quite small. The Yugoslavs themselves are more interested in the frescoes than the building. These were preserved to some extent by nineteenth century frescoes that covered the old ones. Now uncovered and somewhat restored they are among the best in their tradition. I find that they do make me think of Giotto, but that's all there is to it, it's not Giotto. There is considerably more personal feeling than I sense in much other work of the period.... depictions of grief and affection.

"I first visited Nerezi with Barbara Massey, an ornithologist. There was a woodpecker that she was especially anxious to see, who walks down tree trunks head first. I sat northeast of the church to draw the apse end, she went off to bird-watch. I heard a woodpecker nearby and there he was, walking down a tree trunk upside down. He stayed around a long time but she stayed away longer and never saw him."

$\Longleftarrow$ Sveti Kliment, Ochrid, from the southwest

Overleaf: Sveti Panteleimon, Nerezi, entrance from the west $\Longrightarrow$

Overleaf: Sveti Panteleimon, Nerezi, view from the northeast $\Longrightarrow$

Nerezi

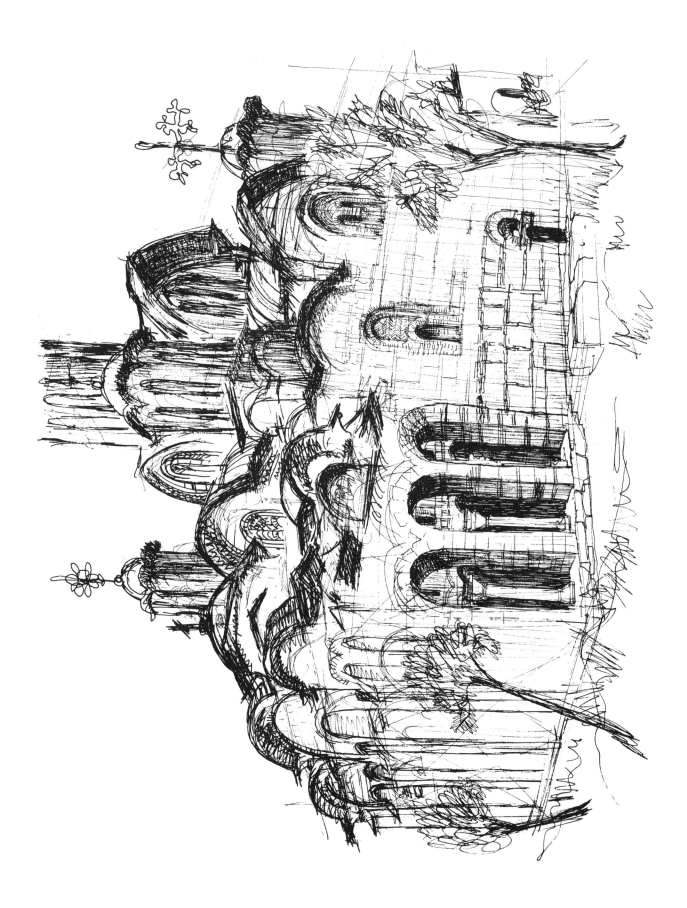

Gračanica

"The single most exciting building in Yugoslavia to me is Gračanica, just outside Pristina. Many towers, domes, and vaults rise in a crescendo of upthrusts calmed by horizontal eaves. It makes me think of early cubism. After three visits I find I am still devoted to this building.

"Though very dark inside, partly because of the added exonarthex, the frescoes are a high point in Yugoslav painting. Fortunately I had a flashlight on my first visit. By 1980 lights had been installed. The portrait of Milutin, King of Serbia, 1282-1321, and founder of Gračanica is in the narthex of the church he founded. He appears bearded and tough, with the slanted eyes that make him easy to recognize. Beside him is his child bride, the Byzantine Princess Simonida. These remain in my mind as a heart-wrenching comment on the complete lack of respect for private life as we conceive it."

The church dates some two hundred years later than that at Nerezi and is an expression of late Byzantine architecture, related to prototypes at Thessalonika. It sits in a meadow, enclosed by a compound of monastic structures. In contrast to its flat site, the building seems to disdain the ground and rises precipitously upward with a multiplicity of domes. All proportions are narrow so as to enrich the feeling of verticality. The dome over the central bay rises to six times its width and the corner bay domes are almost eight times their width.

Gracanica, Church, view from the northwest

⇐

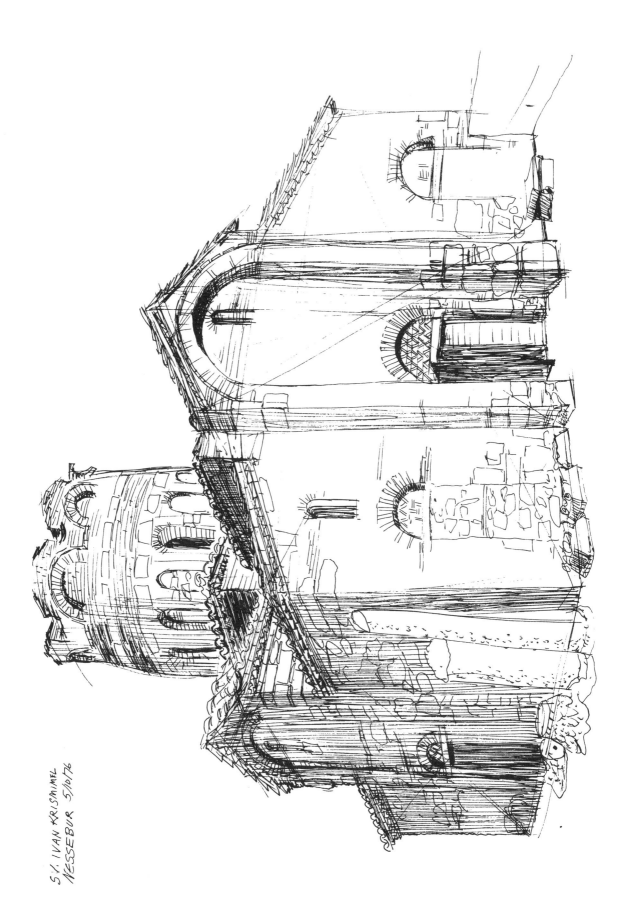

SV. IVAN KRISIMMEL
NESSEBUR 5/10/76

BULGARIA

The First Bulgarian Empire spread quickly over what is now southern Yugoslavia and Bulgaria in the late eighth century. What is known of the architecture of the First Empire has been found through archaeology at the sites of the palace and church at Preslav as well as smaller buildings there and at Pliska. At Nessebar, however, on the Black Sea Coast of Bulgaria, there remains a treasure trove of churches dating from the tenth century to the fourteenth, possibly as early as the sixth century. Some of these represent the height of the Second Bulgarian Empire during the twelfth and thirteenth centuries. There is great variation because of the evolution of forms through this long period but the changes accord with developments at Constantinople as well as in provincial areas of the Balkans.

Nessebar

"My explorations were leisurely, the peninsula is only eight hundred fifty meters long and three hundred wide. The old Metropolitan church is an open ruin with an apse and nave, aisles and a suggestion of galleries. It may date originally from the sixth century but was redone, perhaps in the tenth. It is somewhat reminiscent of St. John Studion in Istanbul, except for the possible galleries. There are great piers still standing and an almost complete apse. While I was there a film was being made in it. An unbearably handsome young couple were to walk from the apse forward. They did it over and over 'til I left. The director was never satisfied.

"Two of the other churches in Nesebar are hardly more than sheds.... but Byzantine sheds with brick and ashlar layering. Sveti Ivan (Saint John the Baptist) possibly late tenth or early eleventh century has a blocky central tower and heavy solid vaults in nave and transepts. It is now a museum."

Sveti Ivan Kristutel, Nessebar, view from the southeast

⇐

93

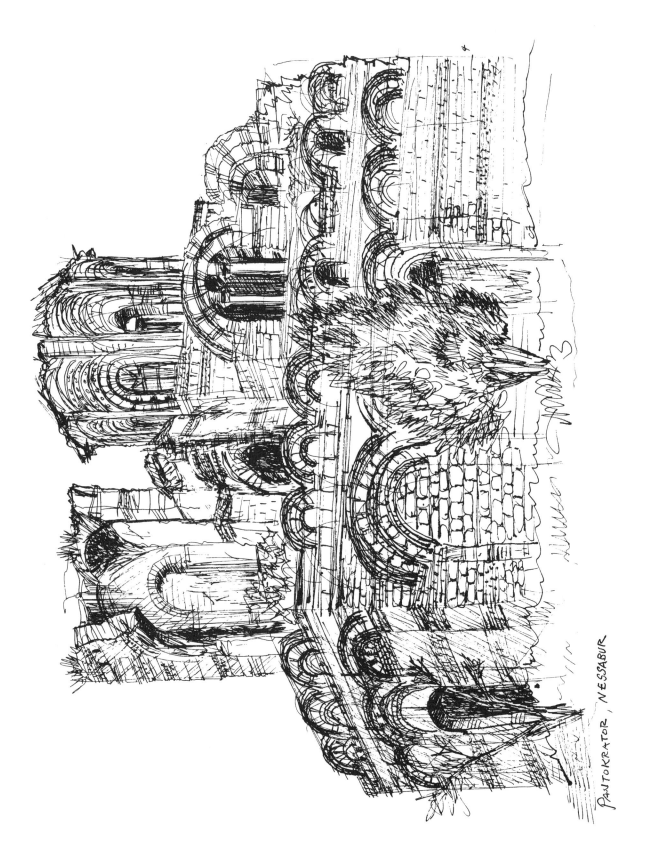

PANTOKRATOR, NESSABUR

"I was able to sit on curbs or handy stones to draw as there were few people about. I had plenty of time and could easily walk to any place on the peninsula so made several watercolors as well as drawings.

"I want to mention that the Bulgarians are big and handsome. At five in the afternoon in Nessebar the world's biggest, rosiest babies come out in English style prams and ride around Pantokrator Church (fourteenth century) in the middle of the town park. I've learned recently that Pantokrator has been restored and is now a museum, as is much of the town of Nessebar."

Church of the Pantokrator, Nessebar, seen from the northwest

⇐

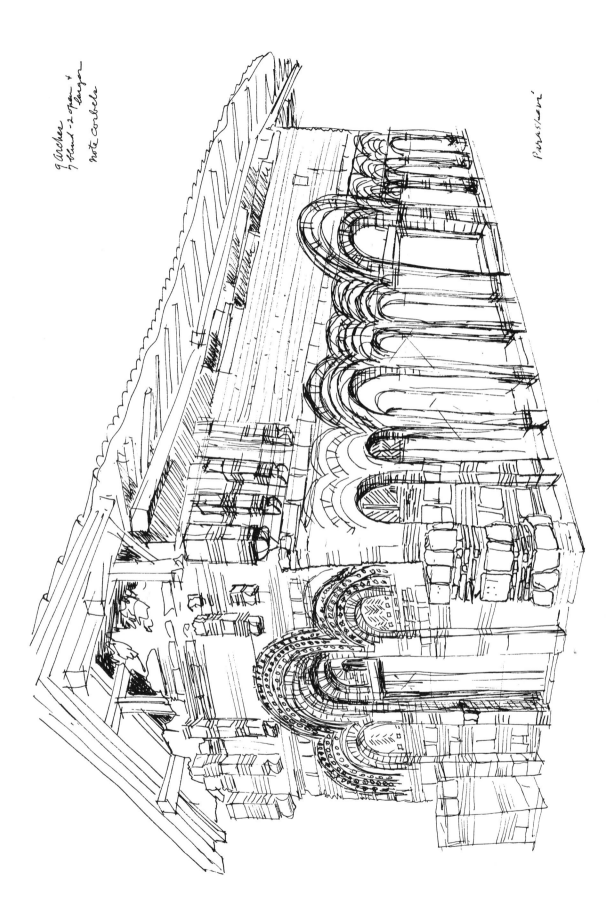

ROMANIA

Romania was at the limits of the Roman Empire when Ovid was exiled there. Rome lost possession of it fairly early in the fourth century. Invaders came and stayed; some passed through but eventually the Vlachs stayed and gave their name to Walachia, the southern province of modern Romania. To the north is the province of Moldavia and to the east the delta of the Danube, the most Romanized territory of all. It was not until the thirteenth century that influence from Byzantium and from Hungary surfaced: Greek from the south, German from the north and west. Walachia and Moldavia were never really Byzantine, but they did accept the Orthodox religion and submitted to various eastern influences in their art and architectural forms, albeit very late relatively speaking.

Princes' Church, Curtea de Arges

Romania can serve as the envoi to these sketches from the Balkans, since it represents the limits in time in the Balkans for Byzantine culture as such. Romania has put on overclothes to prove it is Byzantine, as for example at Curtea de Arges, an early capital of the Vlachs in Walachia. The Prince's church, founded in 1360 by Bassaraba the Great, rears up like a true Byzantine central type structure. Close inspection shows that the masonry is not Byzantine nor are the proportions which seem somewhat awry or top heavy. Not until the sixteenth century did the region of Romania find a renewed creative power and wealth. She was always a prey between Russia and Turkey with the European powers, particularly Austria, kibitzing meanwhile.

Church of the Sucevita Monastery

The Church of the fortified Monastery of Sucevita was built and decorated about 1580 by the Princes of this region of Moldavia, the Movita. It is like a resume of Romanian religious architecture of the sixteenth century and has only a few Byzantine reminiscences, being now an example of architecture unique to Romania.

As had become the custom, the exterior and interior were frescoed. This may account for the extraordinarily emphatic eaves, which have protected the wall paintings these four hundred years. The mixture of stylistic elements includes the pointed Gothic arches of the entrance porch. The tall tower detaches itself from a square base, surmounted by another base starred in shape. It separates out (a bit exaggerated by Catharine but not much) from the architectural mass as do the three apses and the nave with their distinct roofs.

The Church is a delight and comes as an exclamation point to Catharine's travels in the Balkans.

⇐   Sveti Paraskivi, Nessebar, from the west. Stabilized with a wooden roof.

Church of the Sucevita Monastery   ⇒

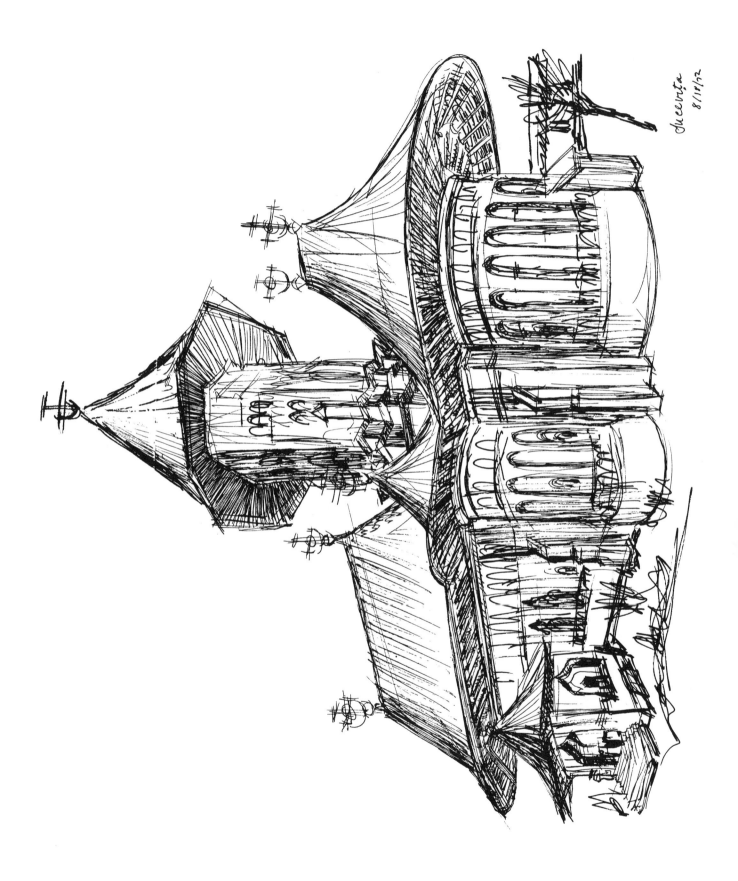

Bucurta
8/18/17

SOME DEFINITIONS

Ashlar	Cut stone masonry.
Barrel-vault	A half-cylindrical vault.
Basilica	Assembly room or church: usually longitudinal, composed of nave and aisles, the former lit by a clerestory.
Cami	A mosque in Turkish.
Corbel	A projecting stone or brick on a wall, that serves as a support.
Drum	The circular or polygonal base for a dome.
Narthex	Vestibule of a church. Inner Narthex: esonarthex. Outer Narthex: exonarthex.
Parekklesion	A chapel flanking the church, narthex or both.
Pendentive	A triangular segment of a sphere resulting from adaptation from a square support for a dome to the roundness of the dome.
Squinch	A small arch or semi-conical niche at the corners of a square bay forming an octagon to carry a dome or a cloister vault.

LIST OF DRAWINGS

102

INDEX

Printed by

Salt River Publishing Services

1990

Editorial Offices at
51 E. 4th Street, Suite 412
Winona, MN   55987